Frank and His Funky Farts

I0528657

Written by
Nicky Gaymer-Jones

Illustrated by
Kaelin Twede

Making Alliteration Fun for All Types!

ISBN: 978-1-964411-05-7 (paperback)

Any references to historical events, real people, or real places are used fictitiously. Names, characters, and places are products of the author's imagination.

Front cover image and book design by Amber Leigh Luecke

Printed in the United States of America

First printing edition 2024

Dedicated to all of the great teachers
who believe in their students.

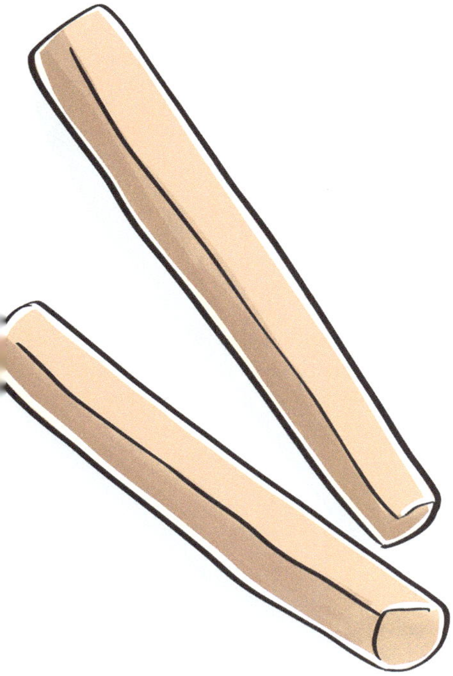

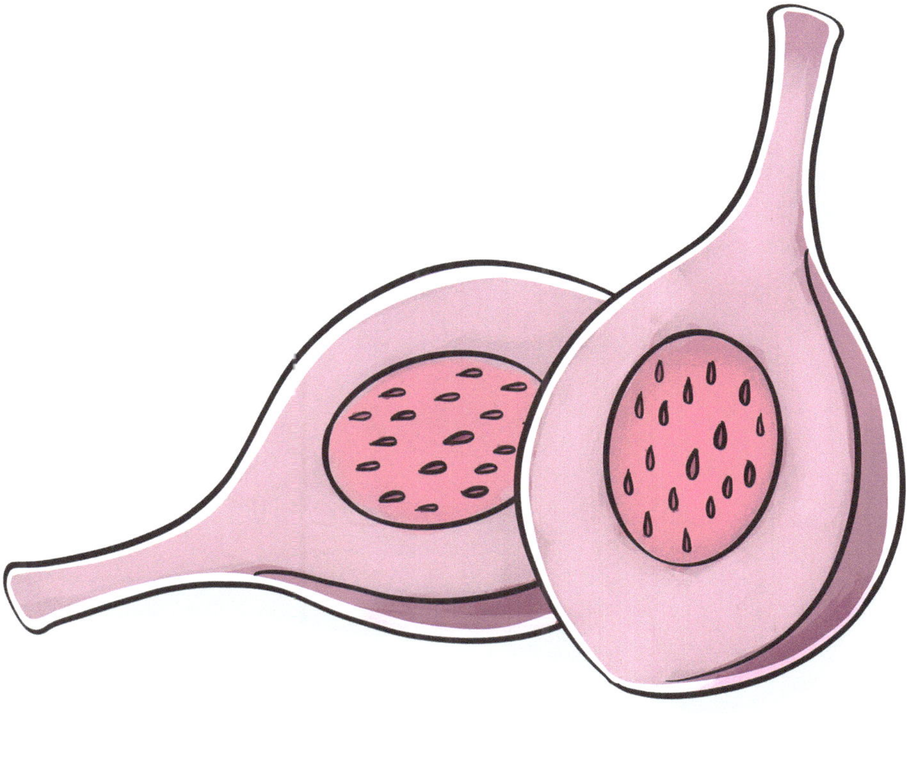

Frank is a funky farter, and he is full of them!
His dad can smell his farts from far,
far away! Frank thinks it is funny that he has
such foul farts, but his dad does not think so.

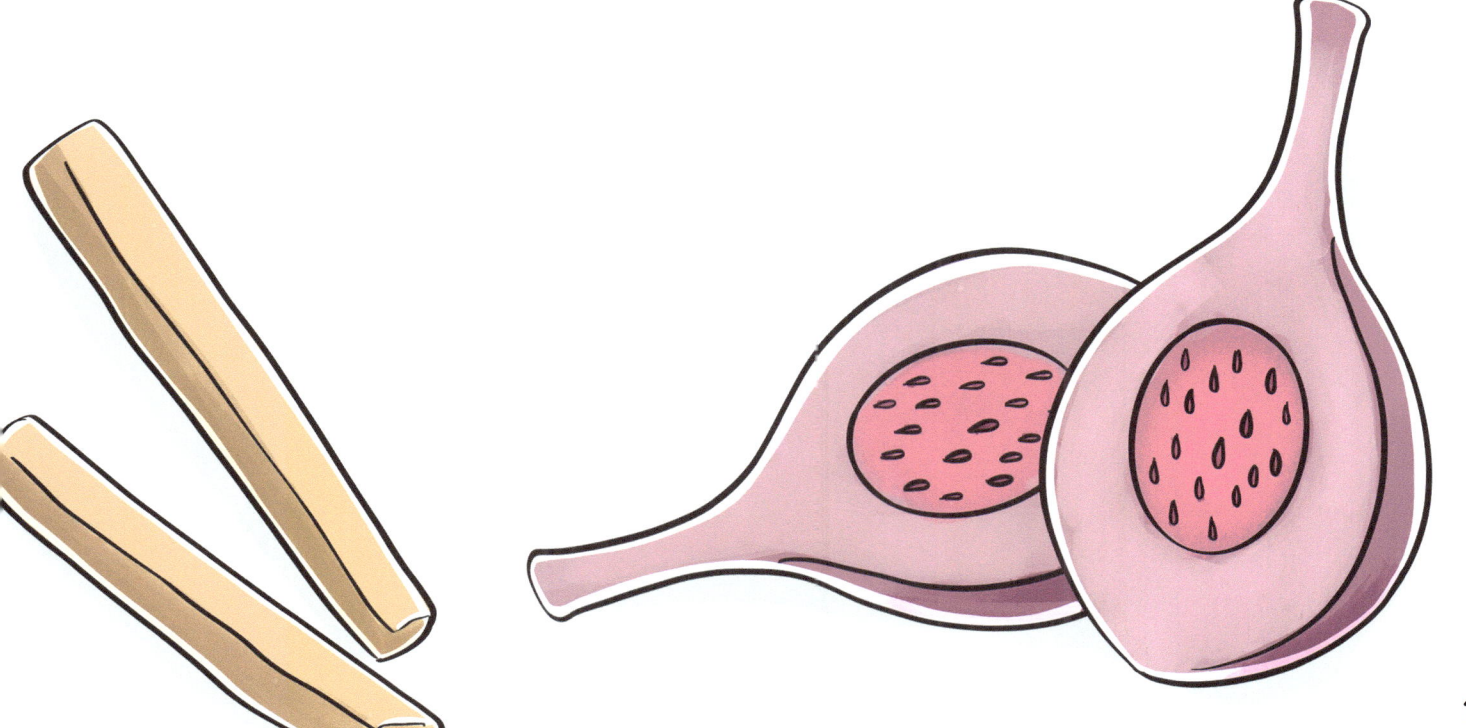

Next Friday comes, and Frank wants to bring his
flute to play for the frog. He also
wants to bring him some frozen fruit, but Frank is
craving French fries. His father buys
him some, even though fries make Frank very farty.

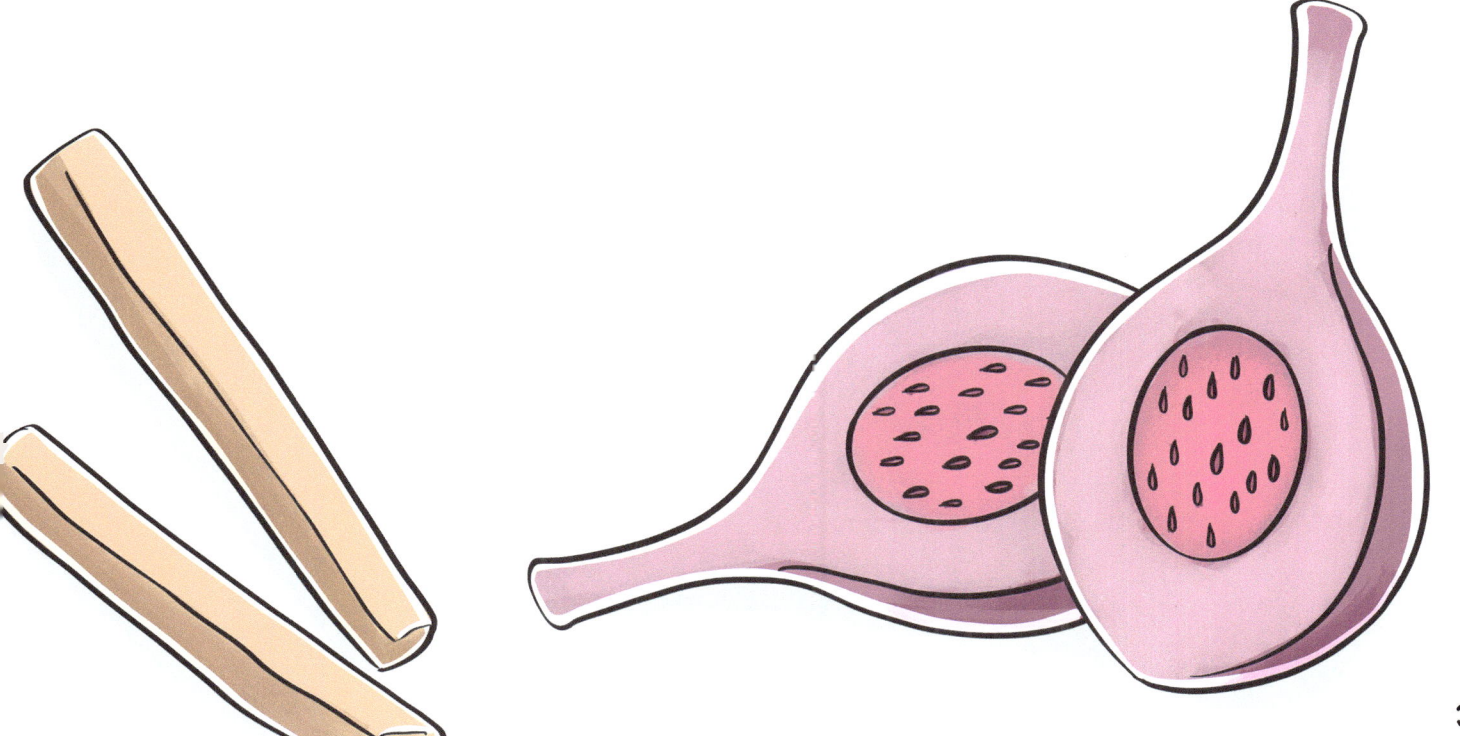

Frank eats his fries and rubs his stomach.

"How do you feel?" his father asks.

"These fries are too much, and now I have to fart!"

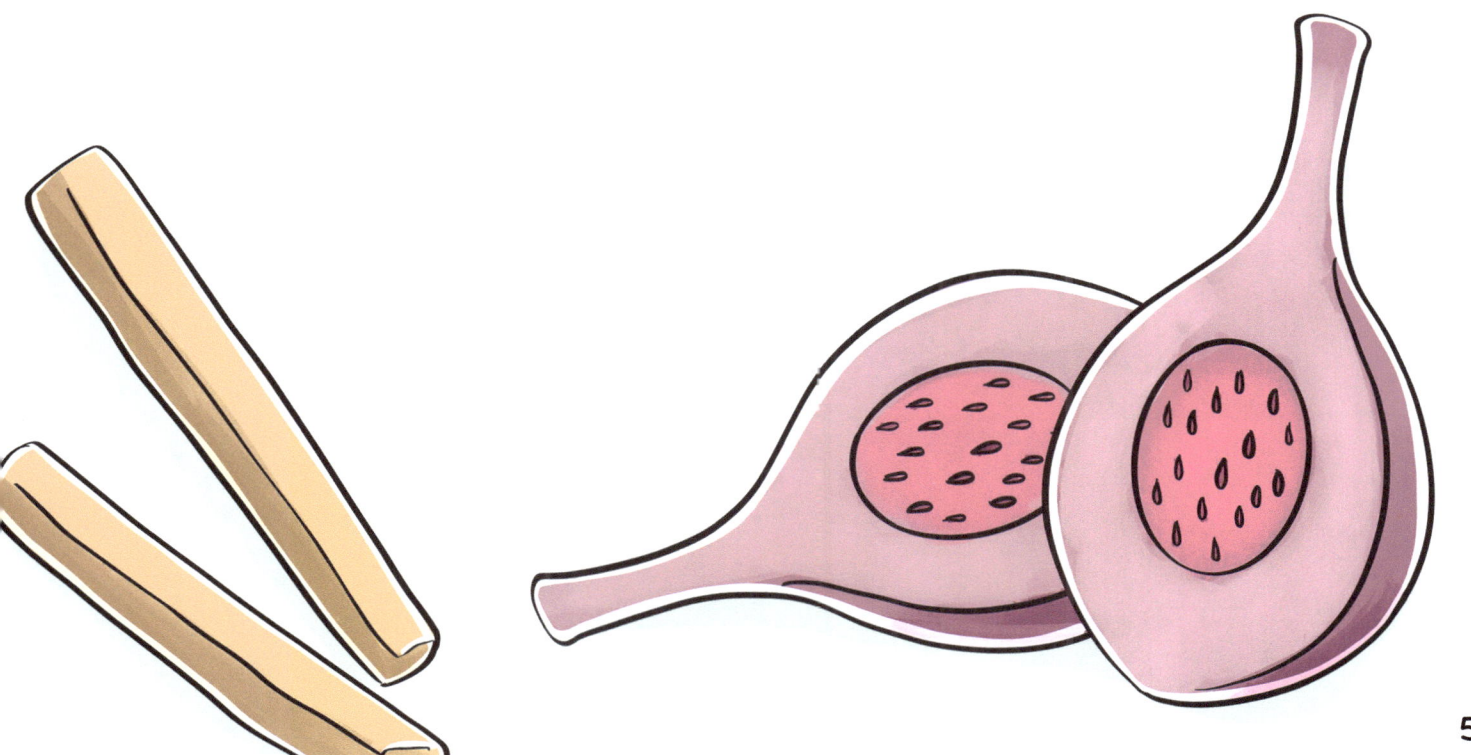

Frank farts in his father's favorite car. His father
covers his nose in fear, but still
thinks it is a little funny. Frank laughs and farts
again. "I think my farts could scare a fox, Dad!"
His father is frightened by Frank's farts and thinks
maybe he needs to fix Frank,
but Frank says his farts are just fine!

"I think we need to take you to the doctor, Frank.
You fart way too much!"
Frank shakes his head. "No, my farts are funny.
They come out fast, and they
smell like a farm. Do not fear my farts, Dad!"

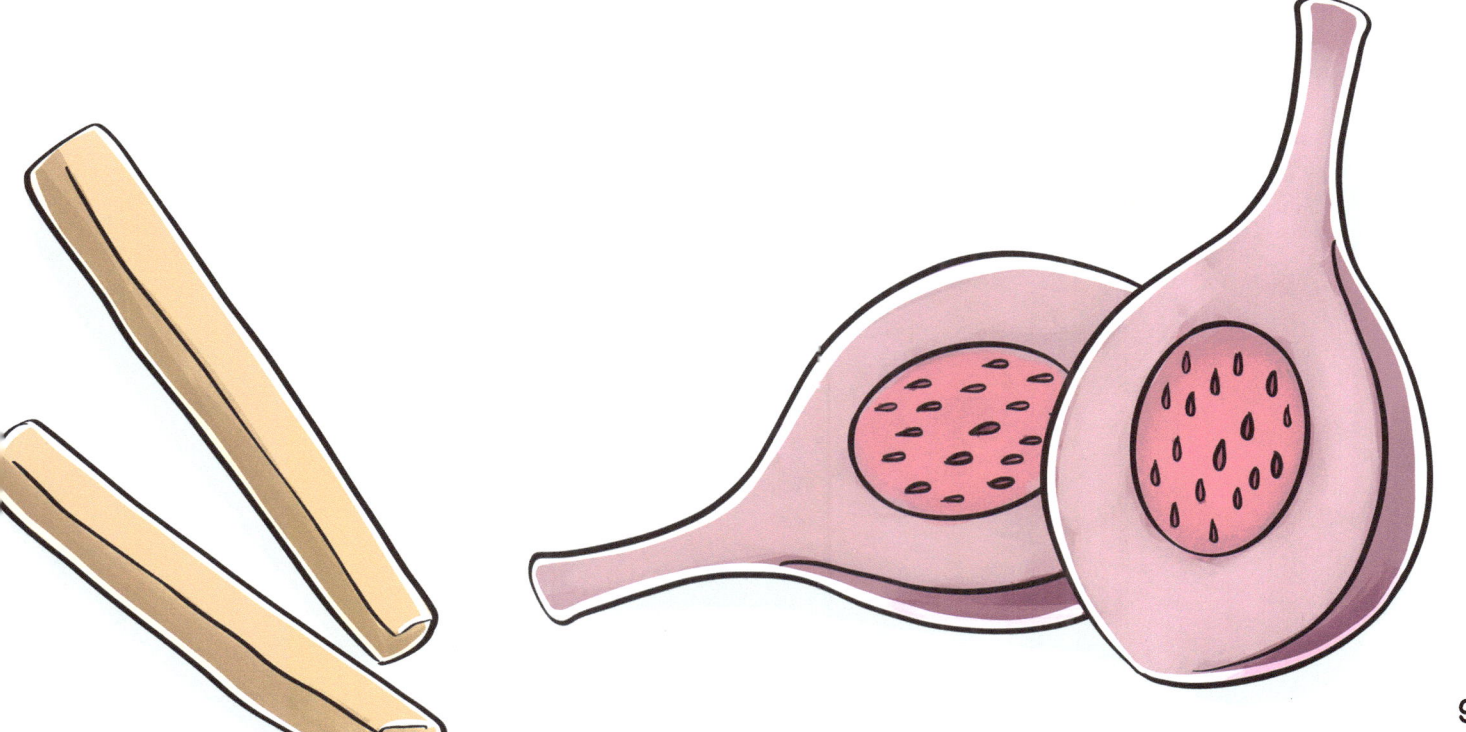

Because it is Friday, Frank goes to his friend's
house and eats lots of fiber-filled
foods like fish, figs, and other fruit. When he
accidentally drops his fork, he farts very loudly!
His friend laughs and pinches his nose.
"We shouldn't have fed you figs, Frank!"
"My farts are fine! They are not that funky!"

Frank is now full of fruit. He cannot eat anymore.

"That was flavorful fruit! I loved it!"

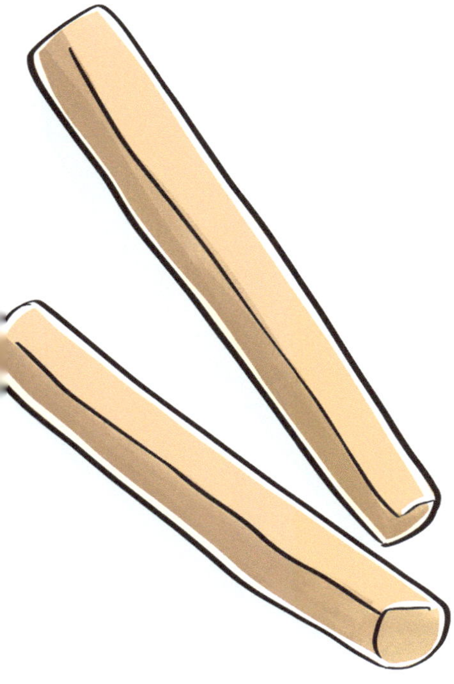

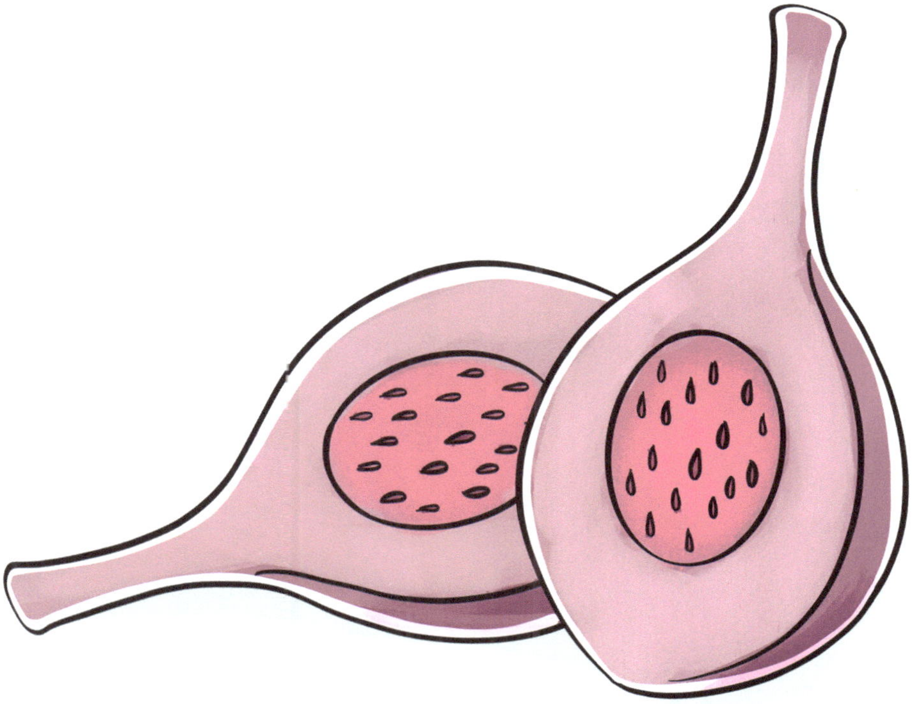

Frank's father is picking him up at five, and Frank
wants to go outside and feel free!

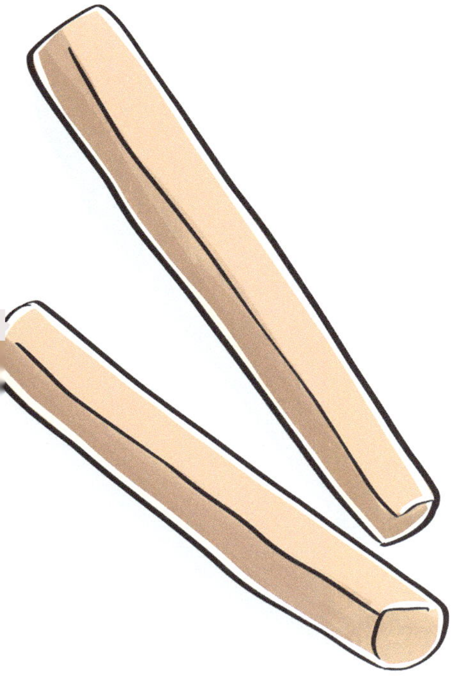

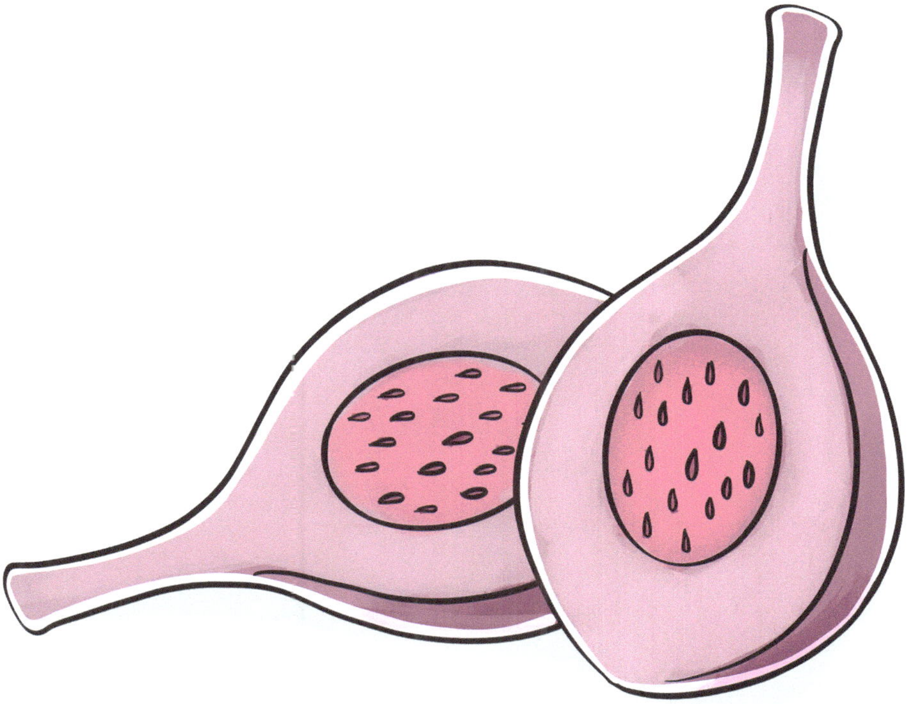

Frank spots a fuzzy frog in the grass.

"Hi, Froggy!" says Frank, "You are very furry. I have never seen such a frog!"

Frank bends over, and his stomach grumbles.

He lets out a fiery fart that makes the frog fly into the air.

"Sorry, fuzzy frog! My farts are like a fireball,
but please don't be scared!"
Frank lifts the frog on his finger and smiles.
The fuzzy frog jumps onto Frank's foot, and
Frank thinks this is very funny!

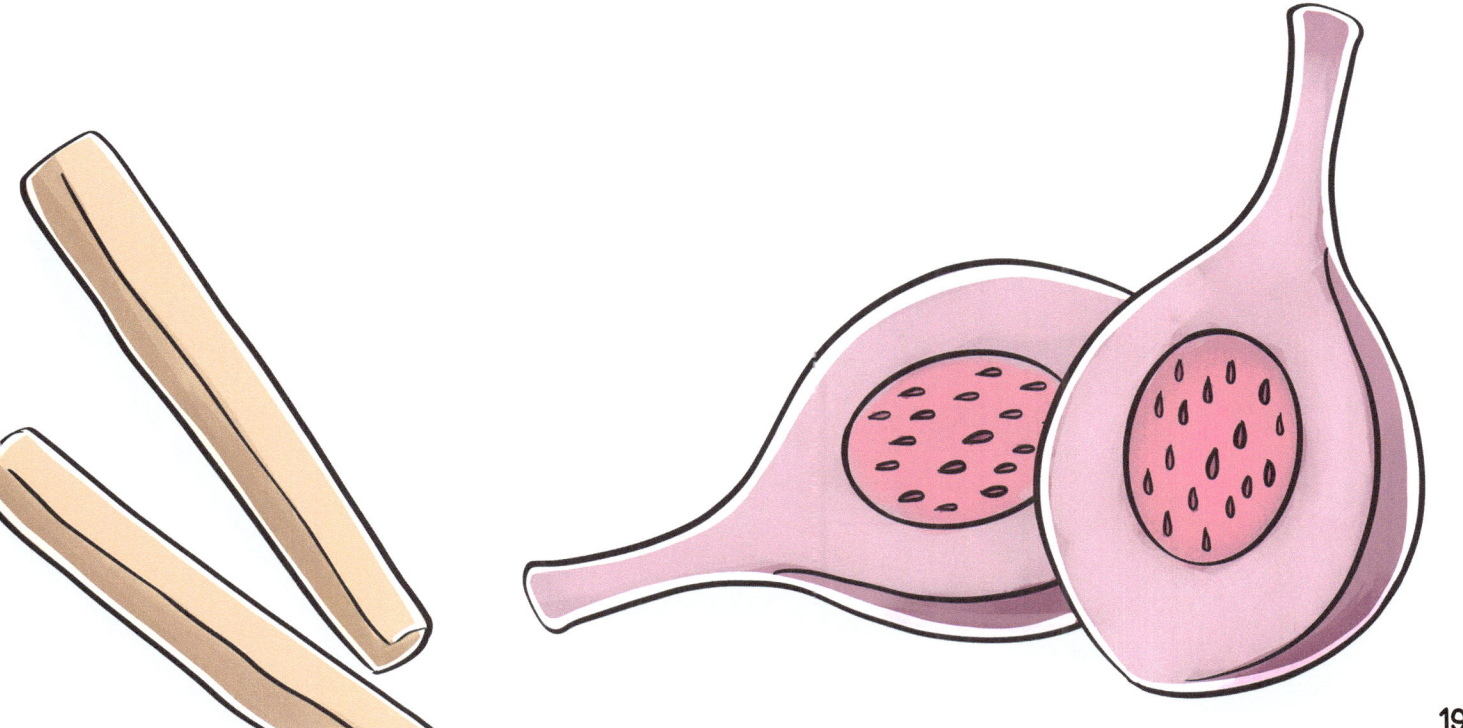

Suddenly, a feather flies in front of Frank and tickles his nose. It makes him fart again!

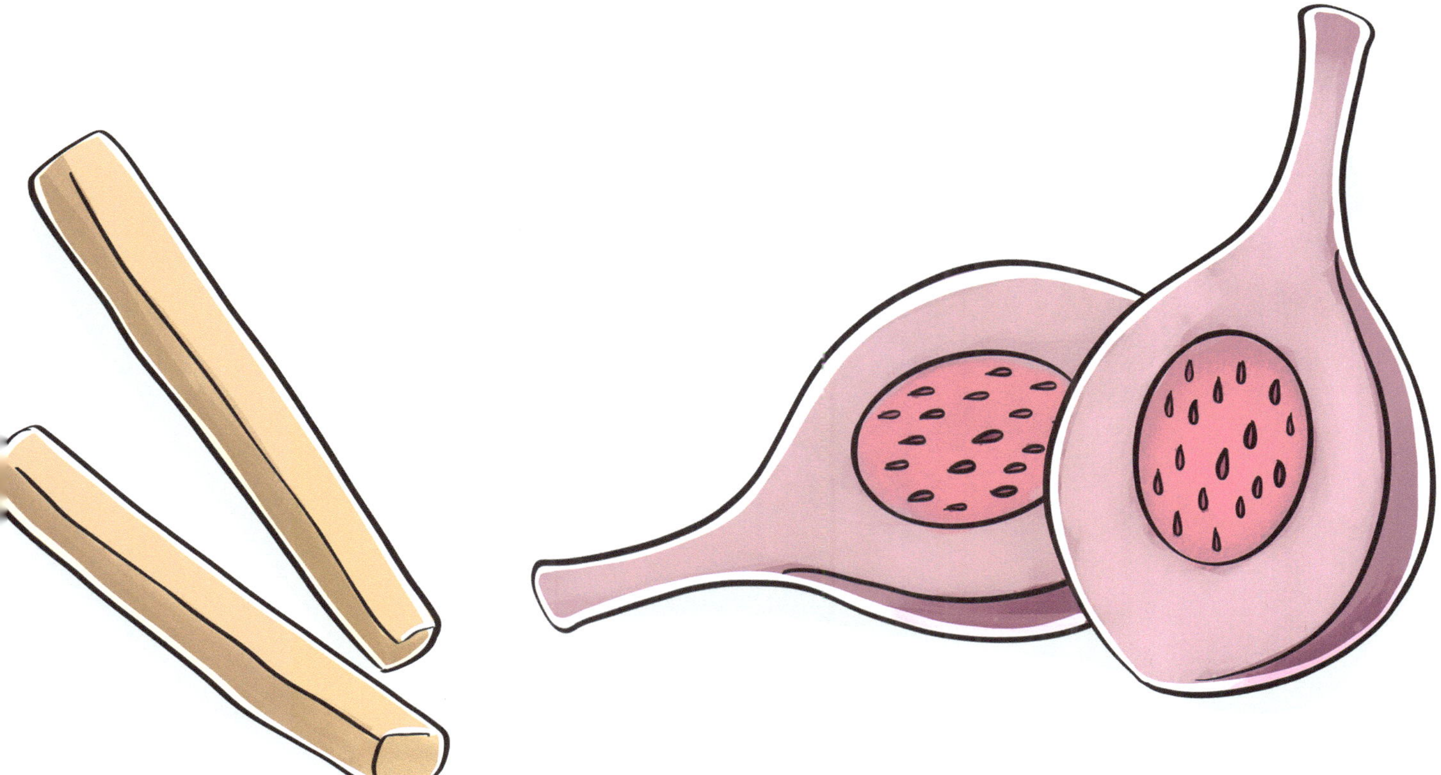

"Sorry about that, frog friend! Can you forgive me?"

The frog croaks and jumps into the grass.

Hopefully, Frank will see the frog every Friday!

Frank's father comes to pick him up. Frank tells his dad that he found a frog friend, and he wants to see him again soon, even if Frank's farts frighten his frog friend.

Discover the Wonders of Alliteration:
A Complete Collection from A to Z!

Dive into a world of wonder and learning with the "Alliteration Fun for All Types" Complete Collection, where each amusing story is dedicated to a specific letter of the alphabet.

From adventurous ants to zany zebras, these captivating tales are designed to engage and empower readers of all types, including those with dyslexia or other learning differences.

This collection of fun stories weaves rhythm, rhyming, and the magic of alliteration to foster a love of reading and promote inclusivity in storytelling.

Whether you're seeking an educational adventure, or inspiring a new reader, this collection promises to captivate young minds and instill a lifelong love for the magic of words.

To learn more visit Nickysbooks.com

If you enjoyed this book, please leave a review on
Amazon and help new readers discover Nicky's books.
Thank you.

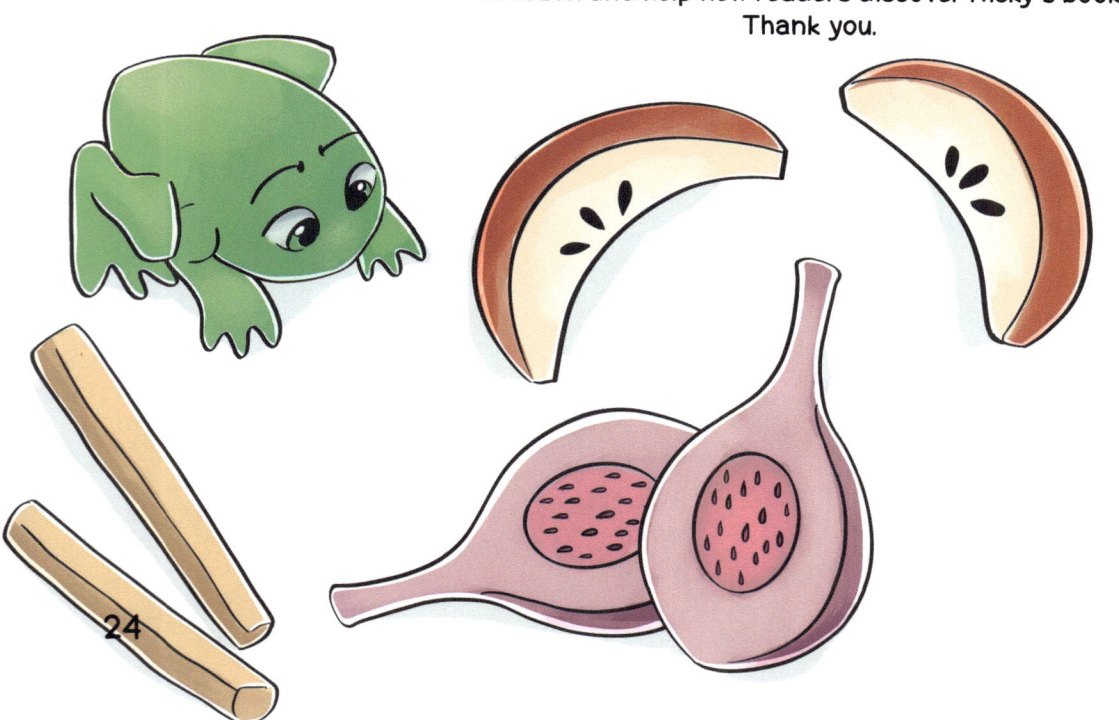

24